THOSE WHO USED THE CORE4 SYSTEM SAY...

Raber's book exposes the shortcomings of The Open Door Policy of employee management utilized in so many organizations today and presents a sound, disciplined, and effective alternative. Core4's practices, implemented in our organization over many years, have shown to be valuable to management and have resulted in a vitally engaged and productive workforce.
—*S. Dale High, Chairman Emeritus, the High Companies*

Thank you, Chet, for writing this book. Having served as CFO of a large subsidiary of a publicly traded corporation, I learned that having the right strategy and business model were never sufficient to achieve success if careful, sustained attention to the human element was missing. Core4 has distilled a set of principles, practices, and skills that should be at the center of any manager's toolbox for getting the job done. This easy-to-read compilation of insights and reports from the field provide an excellent understanding of humane employee management.
—*Gerald Gorelick, former CFO, HealthAmerica*

My observation has been that the most important aspect of the Core4 practices is that it results in employees being empowered—not controlled. Because members were a part of the decision-making process, they made the organization attractive to others. We had little problem filling vacancies when they occurred. This book goes to the heart of the four best practices for the management of people. It's profound yet practical.
—*Norm Kauffmann, Town Manager, Shipshewana, Indiana, Retired; Management Consultant*

An essential element of success that is frequently missing in so many organizations is a humane systems approach to guiding and developing people. Core4 provides that vital humane system. We started using Raber's program in the late '80s, and we observed the tremendous value of his collaborative approach to decision making. Living Branches Retirement Community has used Core4's practices to find the best solutions to challenges and opportunities for our organization, and it is a keystone of our success.

—*Edward Brubaker, President / CEO, Living Branches Retirement Communities*

When used with discipline and openness, Core4's practices help organizations deliver more fully on their missions. The four practices of the system support individual team members to engage, bringing their best to the organization. Core4 is both simple and practical and builds a collaborative and engaged workforce.

—*James Landis, Management Consultant*

(Core4) has allowed all employees to have a voice in our decision making process, which we believe has built trust. The inclusion of Key Performance Measures in our reporting has enabled us to clearly target and monitor accountabilities. In short, the Core4 management system has taken our firm to the next level in our ongoing organizational development.

---*Heather H. Fenimore, Partner, retired, Markley Actuarial Services, Inc.*

I attribute much of the company's success to the management style, Core4, which you introduced to us in the early part of my career. The strong emphasis on team management and also maintaining good one-on-one relationships with individual employees has been probably the most helpful and influential advice I've ever received.

---*Maynard Sauder, retired owner of Sauder Woodworking*

The results for our organization have been evident through a greater sense of fulfillment, higher levels of productivity, and an increasing sense of "ownership" by employees throughout the company. This greater sense of fulfillment has been accomplished by clearly defining performance measures, creating one-on-one time between each manager and every employee on their team, and using the team approach to overcome the challenges that are a part of business each and every day.
---Samuel R. Beiler, former President and COO, Auntie Anne's

THE CLOSED DOOR POLICY

THE CLOSED DOOR POLICY

VITALIZING PEOPLE MANAGEMENT FOR THE TWENTY-FIRST CENTURY
CORE4

Chester A. Raber, PhD

With special assistance by
James E. Fricke, PhD

ISBN-13: 9781535163736
ISBN-10: 1535163739

CONTENTS

INTRODUCTION

One day, sitting under an apple tree, Isaac Newton was hit on the head by a falling apple. That simple event started him thinking more deeply about the concept of gravity, and from that came great contributions to science and human life.

I was also hit "in" the head—not by an apple but by shock as I observed people in organizations and listened to the stories they told.

Our world has brilliant technical creativity. The changes of the last fifty years could not have been anticipated at the middle of the last century (such as portable devices that connect you not only to people but also to the entire universe of world knowledge). Despite these amazing technological advancements, I discovered, surprisingly, that the management of human beings is highly dysfunctional, and even at times inhumane, both in profit-making and in nonprofit companies. The leaders of these organizations were, for the most part, good people who lacked understanding of organizational dynamics and what human beings need to achieve good results and find personal fulfillment.

The result of my observations was the development of the people-management system Core4. The system has been integrated into more than seventy-two organizations over a period of thirty years. The system is logical, relatively easy to implement, and promotes an improved work environment that appreciates its workers as worthwhile human beings as well as contributors to the good results of the organization. Core4 makes a difference!

The exceptionality of Core4, as you will see, is its applicability to organizations of all sizes: from the twenty-person nonprofit early education program to the company that employs thousands of persons in the manufacture of structural steel. Core4 makes a difference!

It is my hope that you will enjoy learning about Core4. I've seen it influence organizations because its conscious effort is to promote humane treatment of the company's most important asset—its employees—while still increasing the good results expected of the organization.

I wrestled with the title of this book. For years, The Open Door Policy has been widely used as a people-management tool. My observation has been that managers think it is an easy way to achieve a better relationship between themselves and their employees, as it is not driven by top-down regimentation. The result, however, is that the organization's management becomes problem driven. The Open Door Policy implicitly states, "Anytime you have a problem, pop into my office, and I'll have an answer." This problem-driven dynamic, operating within organizations that support an open-door policy, has a tendency to relegate important agenda concerns (next steps, plans for the future, and teamwork) to the background.

Furthermore, I have observed that managers and employees really do not like The Open Door Policy. Managers wonder why employees cannot solve their own problems, and employees do not want to admit that they are not able to solve problems on their own. The Open Door Policy, I believe, represents poor management. It is time consuming, demeaning to all, and nonproductive.

Core4 is based on the premise that an employee should not need to have a problem in order to realize important face time with his or her manager or supervisor. Core4 typically uses monthly one-on-one meetings with the supervisor that are dedicated to discussing the progress the employee is making on his or her individual performance plan. These one-on-one sessions with the supervisor, usually held in an office where interruptions are limited to emergencies, are designed to be person focused rather than problem focused. The employee shares with the manager his or her achievements over the past month. This becomes an exciting and rewarding experience as opposed to a defensive or uncertain interaction.

Naming the book *The Closed Door Policy* might be perceived as a blatant attempt to get attention. It was. Now that I have your attention, I hope that you will look beyond the title and see the value in the Core4 system.

Tremendous changes have occurred in our country's history for the improvement of human life. Slavery was abolished, the role of women has changed dramatically, and great strides have been made in medicine and education. Improvements in housing, food, and transportation have made our lives easier and safer. Changes in the workplace—safety, mechanization, and computerization—have all contributed to improved working conditions. Unfortunately, the management of people has not realized corresponding, urgently needed, change. People management is not much different than it was fifty years ago. It is time for change. Core4 can help show the way.

Throughout this text, the word *organization* will be used extensively and in a broad sense as an entity that employs people. Therefore, this definition includes Microsoft as an organization in the same way as a local, unincorporated, nonprofit day-care center is an organization. *Employer* will be used interchangeably with *organization*.

People who are employed by an organization will be referred to in two ways: in some cases as *employee* and other times as *team member*. The term *employee* might seem to minimize an individual's value to the organization, which would be inconsistent with Core4's philosophy. *Team member* suggests a more important role for the individual in the organization. Thus, the terms *employee* and *team member* will be used interchangeably so as to add variety to the written text.

One phrase that will be used throughout the text requires clarification. *Clinical training* is, by definition, "Of or relating to the observation and treatment of actual patients rather than theoretical or laboratory studies" (*Oxford Dictionaries*). The phrase is most often used in psychology, medicine, and other people-related disciplines and has to do with the hands-on training of learners by direct observation of the instructor/coach. In the context of Core4, learners are all managers/supervisors of the organization. The instructor/coach can be a consultant brought in for this special task or an employee who develops the skills as an empathetic observer of personal interactions. (Clinical training of top management, however, is best done by an outside consultant.) The observation and coaching of the learner by a manager is the hands-on process. The coach will observe the learner as he or she conducts team meetings and meets with team members in one-on-one sessions. The development of this clinical training is realized when supervisors/managers comfortably listen, question, coach, support, and encourage their team members.

Chester A. Raber, PhD

CHAPTER 1

HOW IT BEGAN

I grew up in Detroit, Michigan. My father was pastor of a small mission church in the center of that large urban city. Over those years of depression and the Second World War, my parents created a community of caring people. My father was a good man. When I was about age twelve, he took me into his confidence and showed me the accounting book where he carefully recorded the $300-per-month stipend from the mission board and the income from the Sunday morning congregation offerings. The expenses for the church and our family were shown on the other side of the ledger. My father was purposeful in showing me this somewhat confidential information, and I became a more willing participant in the church chores and responsibilities asked of me. I recognized that I was a member of a team.

Twelve years later, in graduate school, I was developing the skills necessary to become a counselor. Our class received lectures, reading assignments, and case studies. Most importantly, however, was the clinical training we received from our skilled professors. We observed a professional staff member dealing one-on-one with a client followed by classroom discussions about what we saw in that session and how we thought the clinician was helping the client.

Eventually, we were assigned clients, and the teaching staff observed us. We were coached gently while being introduced to the skills of listening, questioning, and then asking more questions. Through the encouragement of our instructors and the support of fellow students, we developed skills as soon-to-be clinicians. Working with people in their time of need is a real responsibility; that clinical training provided a confidence base for us budding professionals.

Clinical training is required in several fields—medicine, dentistry, law, and many technical trades—and I reflected on how dangerous and primitive it would be if professionals had not received the clinical training and accreditation necessary for the development of skills vital to their professions. Learning from books is important. Learning through hands-on experience is critical.

I worked for twenty-five years in personal counseling, where I observed many people who continually made poor decisions because they were fearful and had little guidance on or support in how to live a good life. Their unrealistic expectations of themselves and others were the result, in part, of inadequate coaching models and lack of training during their growing years. They had few intuitive memories that guided them to get along in the world of work, marriage, or parenting. Despite these handicaps, my counselees were good human beings seeking to find joy and success in their personal and family lives.

One of the enjoyable experiences I had was working with counselees in group therapy as they struggled to learn from and support one another in their successes in and failures at making changes. The group members did not know—and sometimes did not like—one another. But three times a week, we got together and talked about life, treatment, families, and contributing to the group.

Making the decision to change my professional life from personal counseling to organizational development was challenging. At the time, organizational development was a new discipline, and there were few university degree programs. However, I was convinced that organizational development was a discipline that could make an important contribution to human development, and I wanted to be a part of that future.

I took courses at various universities and learned the history, development, methods, and problems associated with managing organizations. We studied both for-profit and nonprofit organizations, and I was impressed with the similarities between the two, even though different motives were both significant and obvious. It was evident that most employees, while they certainly needed compensation, were fulfilled not by monetary gain primarily but by a desire for achievement and satisfaction, realizing personal goals as they teamed with others to achieve the organization's objectives.

I made that change in my professional life and continued to work at a mental health clinic but positioned my role as consultant to organizations that sought assistance as they made changes and grew.

YOU WOULD THINK THERE WOULD BE A WAY

A counselee told me he was the owner of a successful manufacturing business that employed one hundred people. He was an interesting, energetic person who was optimistic about his company's future. He had made an appointment to see me that morning because he was frustrated with and anxious about persistent trouble with his employees.

"How do you see the problem?"

"Well, for one, my vice president resists my orders. He thinks he has a better way or wants to improve on my plan."

"Oh, what then?"

"I have to lean on him to get him to follow my plan."

"Why don't you fire him?"

"He's a very good vice president and has been with me a long time. I can't fire him. I thought you could help me be more persuasive. He's not the only one. Nobody seems to like how I plan the work, and I get lots of suggestions that won't work."

I listened, trying to understand him and his situation, made several specific suggestions about how to improve communication, and then set another appointment for two weeks later to review the results.

That same day, I had an afternoon appointment with a man also unknown to me. He told me that he was the vice president of a successful manufacturing company that employed about one hundred people, and he described the future as looking good for him personally and for the company. It became clear that my morning appointment was this man's boss. I didn't divulge that information.

He described his boss as constantly controlling every aspect of the organization, while good ideas coming from employees at all levels of the company were ignored. It was a good interview, and I suggested several approaches he might try.

I reflected on these two hardworking, honest men, both with the same goal. They wanted to be successful and tried to make things happen in a positive way, and yet they were in constant conflict. It is one thing if people are in conflict about the business's goals and direction—but these two men agreed on basic issues. I thought there must be some way to resolve this problem. Among many other observations, these two men did not understand human motivation and how organizations work.

Over the next years, I visited many for-profit businesses and nonprofit organizations and sat in on management meetings. When I saw the competition, fear, ridicule, prejudice, anxiety, distrust, and hatred that permeated many of these meetings, I frequently thought that these management teams needed group therapy. I had believed that organizations would be better at dealing with their people. After all, the word *organization* means people working together toward a common goal. Unfortunately—and all too frequently—that was not the case.

Technology is racing forward at a rapid pace as we move into the fifth decade of computer utilization. The need for real, honest, collaborative, face-to-face communication seems to be short circuited—and often misinterpreted—by digital intercourse. As a result, information technology has become a critical component in most organizations. The way organizations manage their people, however, has not kept up. Management/supervision is about the same today as it was fifty years ago.

You might suggest that human resources is the recognized department for dealing with people management. Without question, human resources serves an important function: insurance, leave time, pension issues, and compliance concerns are important and require significant effort. However, human resources is not in a position to confront management about its authoritarian approach in dealing with employees. Top-down authoritarianism—whether benevolent authoritarianism or not, recognized or not—is the norm for the most part.

This is not to say that organizations do not care about their employees or that bad people run them. Rather, it seemed to me, it was the absence of a *system* to oversee and train people for the management/supervision of individuals and teams that had not developed adequately. Not only was there a lack of training but also an almost denial of the need for training those individuals responsible for the management of people in the organization.

WHO AM I TO TELL THEM HOW TO MANAGE THEIR PEOPLE?

A national, rapidly growing snack food company had very specific methods for managing their finances, and they were conscientious of the consistency and accuracy of reporting those financial activities. However, that same organization had no methodology for managing employees. Managers did what was "right in their own eyes."

"What if you allowed every manager to budget, spend, and report finances however they saw fit?" I asked.

"That would be terrible. It wouldn't work. We wouldn't allow it."

"And yet if some of your managers are authoritarian and others are casual, then the people in your company are confused and unsettled."

"Who am I to tell them how to manage their people?" she said. "I don't know how myself."

Managing people may be more difficult because it is personal and can be emotional, whereas managing finances, manufacturing processes, or workplace safety is less so. Fear and a lack of understanding can dominate human interactions. When employee management is inconsistent, resentment, anxiety, and lack of productivity persists.

After observing hundreds of for-profit and nonprofit organizations, I became aware of three outdated operational structures that were still in use in most organizations.

1. Most organizations still operated with an unwanted authoritarian management philosophy.
2. Organizations did not employ a consistent system for people management.
3. Management/supervision was not considered a profession that required training and standards; it was a job that meant increased status and money.

Looking at the first of these outdated operational structures, it was apparent that most organizations, be they profit or nonprofit, are managed through an authoritarian chain of command. Authoritarianism has a long history as the basic method of organizing and leading, whatever the size or type of organization. Militaries, churches, and businesses are the same in this regard. Whenever and wherever organizations were established and for whatever end product, leadership created the group's purpose and went about hiring people to carry out their stated goals.

Our earliest authoritarian leaders were fathers, priests, clan leaders, kings, emperors, and popes. Now we have owners, presidents, boards, and managers. All lead with an authoritarian philosophy, consciously or not.

Authoritarian control over a person's life was accepted as normal in the historical context. Humans feared and submitted to kings, plantation owners, and now managers/supervisors while longing for more freedom and self-expression. In those early centuries, workers were unable to break the ties of authority without facing certain economic doom or even death. Change was slow but inevitable. Domination by authority kills incentive, creativity, motivation, fulfillment, and joy.

In the current world of work, 90 percent of the leaders and workers I polled said they do not like or want authoritarian leadership. Leaders of most organizations recognize this antipathy toward authoritarianism but do not know how to move in a new direction. Instead, they struggle with short-term fixes.

Some short-term fixes have included The Open Door Policy, Situational Leadership, The One Minute Manager, talk with your people, have more meetings, and The New One Minute Manager. Organizations have used numerous personality assessments that attract attention and result in group activity that may help. However, these short-term approaches do little to improve the management of people.

One common management style being used today, The Open Door Policy, suggests that any time an employee has a problem, he or she can pop into the manager's/supervisor's office, and an answer will be readily available. This is a problem-based management system in which the leader's time and energy are given to solving problems, many of which should not have occurred in the first place. An open-door policy is a feeble attempt to cover up authoritarianism.

I HAVE AN OPEN DOOR POLICY

"I have an open door policy," were a hospital executive's exact words when I asked about his management style.

"What does that mean?"

"If anybody has a problem, then they're free to come by my office at any time."

I asked him how the policy was working. He described numerous walk-ins every day and sometimes until eight o'clock at night.

"Have you suggested to employees that they might do some problem solving on their own?"

"I've sometimes wondered why these workers couldn't figure out answers to their problems for themselves, but they want to know what I think. I do get to know what's going on within the organization, and it keeps me on my toes."

The open door policy may not be strictly authoritarian, but it is problem focused. Managing problems (errors) is not leadership. It's more like fixing flat tires all day long. Leadership involves looking to the future and supporting and encouraging workers as they meet the challenges of task accomplishment on a daily basis.

The problems stemming from and the energy required to cope with the subtle evils of authoritarianism are clearly seen in the movie *The Stanford Prison Experiment*. This movie was based on the work of Philip Zimbardo who, in 2007, published *The Lucifer Effect*. The Stanford experiment revealed the problems that develop when authoritarianism is allowed and becomes the rule. The author subtitled his book *Understanding How Good People Turn Evil*.

Authoritarianism is so pervasive and so much a part of the standard operating procedure that most managers are unaware of its demoralizing effects on employees, even though they may feel it in their own relationship with their managers.

The second outdated operational structural deficiency, which I identified in my observation of both profit-making and nonprofit organizations, was the absence of any system, much less a humane system, for the management of people who work for that company. The word *system* implies that, throughout the organization, supervisors/managers relate to all of their employees in a similar way.

Humane people management can help prevent situations such as the following.

NOBODY KNOWS WHAT I DO

I was sitting in the waiting area outside the office of a college president. I observed of the secretary with whom I had previously become acquainted, "You're very busy today."

"I'm always busy, but nobody knows what all I do. Not only that, but I don't think anyone appreciates what I do. I never hear a thank-you."

"Oh?"

"Stuff gets dumped in my inbox, I do it, and I return it to their inboxes. I am the go-to person for getting things processed for four men who stay behind closed doors. I'm not told the background of the material I'm working on. I might as well be a machine. I have no idea where I belong. I'm not on any team."

I observed that it is not uncommon for even educated, well-intentioned leaders to be unmindful of their staff and ignore their needs to be a real part of the process and a value to the organization. Frequently, leaders hire someone just to do a job and not be a part of the team. Employees can work for many people if they have a good, clear relationship to their supervisor and their team. Many company presidents, leaders, and managers seem unaware of the human needs and values of the people who work for them, and consequently, they manage them inadequately.

WHY DOESN'T SHE SMILE?

At one local organization where I visited regularly, I became acquainted with the very busy receptionist. We had good, brief conversations.

"I never see you smile," I gently whispered.

"There's nothing to smile about."

"What do you mean?"

"Nobody tells me anything. They just give me work. My boss doesn't know all that I do, and no one smiles at me. I don't like working here, and I'm trying to find another job."

People have a need to belong, to feel appreciated rather than isolated, used, and alone. It is hard to feel good about what you do under conditions like these.

It is not just the support staff who can suffer from the absence of a humane system for people management, as the following story illustrates.

I CRIED

A vice president of a local manufacturing company had a good reputation in a growing, successful business.

"How are things going at work?" (*We were casual friends.*)

"We had a staff meeting yesterday, and it made me very uncomfortable. Again, the president called all the vice presidents together—no agenda and no prior notice. These meetings can last from thirty minutes to ten hours. Yes, ten hours!"

"What happened yesterday?"

"It was like other meetings. The president was angry about something one vice president was supposed to have done, and he took four hours of our time to beat up that guy in front of the rest of us. It was terrible."

"Have you ever been the target of those attacks?"

"It happened once, three years ago. He hasn't done it to me since."

"Why?"

"I cried." (*Silence.*) "I was embarrassed, he was embarrassed, and all of the other vice presidents were embarrassed. We were speechless. That was the last time he attacked me."

"How do you and he relate now?"

"It's like walking on eggshells. He hints at things, and I try to understand his message. Everyone in the company's uncomfortable with him, but we can't afford to rock the boat."

I was not really shocked by this story. I had heard similar stories from the workplace. It no longer surprised me how leaders failed to get it, but then, they had little or no training in managing people. They fail their owners, customers, employees, and themselves with their poor relationships and problem-solving methods. Everyone loses when leaders fail to understand how organizations work and the dysfunction they cause when employees are criticized publicly and even in private. Criticism is outdated authoritarianism, whereas coaching, training, and support build results and relationships.

Unfortunately, failure to deal with their team members happens all too often. In the following story, the supervisor had no concept of how his actions were going to be interpreted by the team.

MIRROR, MIRROR

I heard a loud voice yelling at someone. I waited until the voice stopped. After another minute, I continued on to the room. Everyone was back at work, and no one looked up when I entered. I had come to consult with the manager, whose voice was the one I had identified as the loud person.

We had been working together for some time and had a good relationship. Even before I had a chance to begin, he asked, "Did you hear me yelling at David? He's been off the reservation for several weeks now, and I felt I had to let him know that what he was doing was wrong."

"Yes, I did hear you. I wondered what was going on."

"He does a lot of things on his own that don't work out. I've told him time and again to stop, but he says his way is easier, and the results are the same. But the results aren't the same."

"Were the other members of your team hearing this 'discussion'?"

"Yes, but I was angry. His defiance has happened too often."

"OK, let's talk about this a little."

"Sure. They certainly saw me leading."

"That might be true, but I guess my question is what did they really see?"

"Well, they saw me laying down the law on following orders."

"Yes, but what else did they see?"

"They saw I was angry. What's wrong with that? I even thought about the other team members as it was going on—I didn't like that they were listening—but I also thought it might be good for them all to know that I'm the one calling the shots."

"How do you suppose David feels right now? How do you think he feels about you?"

"I guess he's angry too."

"Yeah, you're probably right about that, but what is he angry about?"

"That I caught him at it again!"

"Or what else, maybe?"

"Well, probably that I jumped on him with others around. I thought about that also as it was happening, but I was already into it."

"I've always thought that a good way to understand these matters is to ask yourself how would you feel if it were happening to you. I call this the mirror, mirror view. How would you have felt if your boss was cussing you out in front of the entire team you work with every day? How would you have felt?"

"Yeah, I'd probably be pretty upset."

"Is that how you want your team to feel about you?"

"No, but I want them to respect me."

"Of course. Do you think they respect you more now than they did before this incident?"

"I hope so."

"Would you have respected your boss if he did that to you?"

"Truthfully, I think I would've hated him."

"Respect and hatred are two very different things. I'll bet the team is afraid of you more now—afraid that they might catch the same treatment if they try any of their own ideas. Is that what you want?"

"No. I want them to try new things but to tell me first and get my approval."

"OK, let's start over. What might you do differently with the same situation facing you?"

"I think it would've been better if I'd talked to him in my office."

"And what else would've been different?"

"I think I should have tried not to get so loud."

"And what would have been your approach?"

"It would've been better to ask him questions rather than to yell at him."

"Why would that have been better?"

"It's kind of like what you're doing with me right now. Approaching him with questions would have allowed me to think rather than to just get mad. Possibly, I could've even gotten him to think about how what he had done caused my concern rather than just getting mad."

"I think you've got it. Your relationship to your team is so valuable that I'm sure you would rather have their respect than their fear."

Criticism is everywhere. Parents, sports coaches, and even teachers are quick to point out mistakes, faults, and failures. Criticism is an outgrowth of authoritarianism, where the attitude is "I'm right, so pay attention to what I tell you." The response to criticism can be fear, defensiveness, and/or withdrawal. How much better it would be if the individual doing the criticism reflected on how it would feel to be on the receiving end of those same words. The supervisor here seemed to have figured it out.

In order to dispel the idea that these stories are representative of a time past, let me share a recent situation.

I DON'T GET ANY

I mentioned to a social worker friend that I was in the process of writing a book about people management in the workplace.

"That's interesting. We have a new people-management push on at our office. My manager said to me at our recent get-together, 'Now what is this? I'm supposed to compliment, praise, and appreciate you. I don't get any of that. Why should I give you any?'"

From this interchange, what do you think are the chances there will be any modification to the management of people working in that organization?

The third outdated operational structure cited earlier had to do with absence of training for the management of the organization's primary asset: human beings. Not a single organization that I observed had training in place that specifically dealt with how managers/supervisors related to the individuals in their charge. To be a manager or supervisor required little recognized training, standards, guidelines, monitoring, or certifications. There was no auditing or monitoring of people management, no procedures to be followed for people management, and no peer-review association as exists in all professional groups.

Top management was no better than lower management in this regard. Experienced, highly paid executives resist even the expectation that supervision is for them as well as for their subordinates. They often operate completely on their own. In some organizations, the chief operating officer can also be the chairman of the board and the company president. Would a person with all of those titles think he or she might need some supervision? Probably not. This leaves the organization vulnerable and liable for unsupervised behavior.

The Peter principle (the observation that people rise to a level of their incompetence) is alive and well in many organizations. If a person excelled in a technical job, then he or she might be moved into a management position: She was an excellent teacher, so why don't we make her a principal?

ONE OUT OF FOUR

A pharmaceutical company contacted me for guidance on a personnel problem. Four senior chemists, all with significant contributions to the company in chemistry, had reached the top of the chemist pay scale. Wanting to keep these individuals, the company promoted them into management positions. These four chemists received increased compensation and status. But three of these promotions were compete failures; only one was successful. After interviewing all four individuals, I made a recommendation to management that seemed so obvious. The skill set necessary to be a successful chemist is not that needed to be a successful manager. Of the four persons, one had exceptional abilities in both areas; the other three did not.

I recommended that the salary range for chemists be increased to a salary level that matched the management salary scale, allowing the three skilled chemists to continue doing what they enjoyed and advance their achievements. The skills and abilities needed to be a manager are often not found in technically oriented individuals.

More importantly, however, the idea that a person can be moved into a managerial/supervisory position with no training for that role is, at best, naive. They had trained for years to be chemists, not managers.

Even when a new employee is hired for a management position, there is often a failure to examine how that individual's practices of dealing with employees were exercised in his or her previous position or what training he or she may have had for managing people.

TWENTY-FIVE YEARS OF EXPERIENCE

I'd been working with a company for several months, and the owner attended all training sessions and seemed to have an understanding of the Core4 approach to people management and the decision-making process. He wasn't at the beginning of that day's session but arrived, excited, for mid-session; it was obvious he wanted to share something with the group.

"I'm happy to report that I've just hired a plant manager!"

The team knew the plant manager position needed to be filled. The owner's unilateral hiring, however, was out of step with the group's previous discussions on how company decisions might best be made but quite in line with his past behavior.

"What are his qualifications?"

"Well, he's got twenty-five years of experience!"

Later, I asked whether the general manager, the owner, and I could talk with the new hire and learn about his management style and training.

After introductions and handshakes all around, I introduced the reason for the meeting and asked, "What is your method for managing your people?"

"I just do it," was his immediate response.

"Do you talk to your people individually?"

"Of course!"

"And when do those meetings occur?"

"Wherever it's needed, whenever there's a problem."

The president and general manager's eyes met as they began to realize that the new plant manager had, at best, a problem-oriented management style.

"Do you have a team, and does the team get together?"

"Yes, we do. Whenever there's a problem, we get together and talk it out."

A problem-oriented management style rather than a people-oriented and problem-prevention management style represents an approach to management that is problematic and least productive. Twenty-five years of implementing a problem-oriented management style can be a difficult pattern to change.

This story is an example of what happens in many organizations. The owner, having no training of his or her own, believes that all managers do what's right in their own eyes. After all, if someone's been doing the same thing for twenty-five years, then how wrong could it be?

When management believes either subliminally or overtly that the sole purpose of work is for workers to earn money, it is difficult for the workers to have much fulfillment or joy. Some supervisors, managers, and presidents are aware of this lack of joy in the workplace based on their own experiences, yet they have little understanding of how to remedy it.

In my assessment of the workplace, it became important to focus on two fundamental questions. First, what does the organization want and need from its employees? Second, what do employees want and need from the organization to do their best work?

Management's needs can be simply put. First, the organization wants good results. If the company is a profit-making business, then the financial bottom line is the payoff. If the organization has stockholders, then the pressure to arrive at good results can be formidable. Employees who are skilled, well trained, creative, and highly motivated are of great value to the organization.

For a nonprofit organization, good results may be more difficult to quantify and often may be a long-term endeavor, making it more difficult for a board of directors to assess the organization's results either accurately or in a regular manner. In these cases, the board relies heavily on the chief executive officer or on hearsay.

But for all organizations, good results are first and foremost. Management believes that good results come from a workforce that is amiable, obedient, skilled, and conscientious.

Management asks the workforce to provide prompt and efficient follow through on its directives. Leadership provides the vision and goals; employees carry out the directives handed down by leadership. This is the authoritarian model at its naked best.

Management also wants a workforce that cooperates with one another through teamwork. While many managers/supervisors and organizations do not really understand teams and how to help teams work effectively, all managers want their employees to cooperate. Sometimes, the supervisor allows or encourages employees to compete with fellow workers, which causes dysfunction, and everyone ultimately suffers.

Next, when assessing employee needs, certain conditions are important, but surprisingly, financial compensation is not that high on the list of those conditions.

Employees say they often do not have but need a clear, agreed-upon assignment that both the manager and the employee thoroughly understand and that both are committed to achieving.

I THOUGHT YOU KNEW

I was in a manager's office talking to him about Core4 when there was a knock on the door.

"Come in."

"Sorry, Stan. I didn't know you had someone here."

"That's all right, Mitch. What's going on?"

"I'll be out this afternoon and just wanted to remind you."

"Thanks. By the way, how is the Smithgal project coming along?"

"No idea. I'm not involved."

"Yes, you are."

"Since when?"

"Don't you remember last month we talked about that situation?"

"I remember the conversation, but I thought you were just informing me. Nothing was ever said about me being responsible."

"I thought you knew. Why else would I take the time to tell you all about it?"

"I did wonder about that. I've got a full load and couldn't take on the Smithgal thing in the middle of the year, even if you had asked me."

"This is a problem! It's an important project, and you're my best guy."

"Sorry. I've got to run. See you on Monday."

The door closed, and the manager said, "I don't know what I'm going to do. Smithgal is critical."

Employees want a clear, agreed-upon assignment. Mitch obviously did not get an agreed-upon assignment and, in fact, was not even aware he had an assignment.

Knowing that circumstances sometime occur during the course of an assignment that require changes, the employee wants to feel confident that the manager understands and agrees to support those changes that they mutually recognize as being needed. Employees say they need a relationship of mutual trust and confidence with their manager as they work together toward the completion of the agreed-upon task.

Employees want to understand and participate in the decision-making process because they feel they can contribute beyond the level of a suggestion box. Employees want to believe in the organization's integrity and values, particularly as they relate to ethics, dedication to community, and working toward world betterment. And finally, employees need to feel that they are being fairly compensated for their efforts.

Many companies have failed to recognize that they have an account-ability to their employees that transcends the confines of the work product, but awareness is growing. In his book *Good Value* (2010), Stephen Green, president of the British Banking Association, stated,

> What is indisputable…is that the way a business engages with its people takes us straight into the realm of sustainability and social responsibility…it is abundantly clear—as any businesses that have regular graduate recruitment programmes will know—that the next generation of management demands to know what the policies of the company are…It means that the company has to be able to ask—and give a satisfactory answer to—the question: How does the business we do contribute to the common good? (173–74)

In his recent book *The Best Place to Work: The Art and Science of Creating an Extraordinary Workplace* (2014), Ron Friedman describes the American workplace in terms similar to those used in this book's first chapters. He offers excellent suggestions on ways to improve the workplace.

> Many of my friends really dread their jobs. They complain about employers who treat them like machinery—there to churn out whatever is required of them, regardless of the cost to their motivation, creativity or personal health. Their bosses seem to expect that they work long hours and stay glued to cell phones at night, but then show little appreciation or, worse, micromanage them. No one likes it; but what alternatives are there when employers have deadlines to meet or products to develop? (Suttie 2015)

Friedman, a psychologist and business consultant, makes commendable suggestions on how small improvements can be made. Some of Friedman's recommendations may come as a surprise to those unfamiliar with the science, and some may even seem downright counterintuitive:

- Companies should encourage failure, which makes risk taking easier.
- Companies should focus on what is going well.
- Companies should empower employees to find their own approaches to getting the job done.
- Employees should have more control (ownership) over their work products.

While these tips and suggestions are certainly useful, they will be of small value unless contained in a well-designed management *system*. The same can be said for some of the outlandish work environments popping up in high-tech companies in the Silicon Valley. Ping-Pong, air hockey, and Smurf basketball are fun, but do they have a place in the work environment? Maybe, but not in the absence of a structured management system such as that offered by Core4.

Early in the labor movement, the union effected workplace change for the betterment of the worker. Safety regulations, minimum age laws, and leave policies were modified, to mention a few. Unfortunately, unionization sometimes led to an adversarial relationship between employees and management. Productivity suffered, profits fell, and the workplace was anything but a joyful experience. For some, the authoritarian mind-set prevailed: "Working is tough. People get hurt, feelings are bruised, people get pushed around, but that's just the way work is." Fortunately, almost everyone recognized there had to be a better way.

In the following chapters, I take you through the four essential practices of Core4, which create a participative management environment that brings improved results for the organization as well as fulfillment and joy for the workers. While it may not solve all company/employee problems (after all, people are people, and anyone may fail to take the high road occasionally), it has been demonstrated that a conscientious effort to follow the Core4 practices can result in measurable benefits for all: owners, managers, and employees.

CHAPTER 2

PEOPLE MANAGEMENT FOR THE FUTURE

In 1903, John Muir, the great American naturalist, invited President Theodore Roosevelt to join him on a visit to Glacier Point in what is now Yosemite National Park. They camped and explored the Yosemite Valley below: El Capitan, Half Dome, and Yosemite Falls. Muir's purpose, in addition to viewing the natural beauty of the land, was to engage and expose the president to the land being despoiled by development. Entrepreneurs built hotels, houses, and campgrounds on the pristine land; ranchers grazed sheep and cattle on the fertile hillsides; hunters slaughtered wild animals with impunity; and the railroad laid tracks into the valley, providing the wealthy easy access to this natural wonder.

Muir's vision was to preserve Yosemite and other areas in the country that were equally as precious in natural beauty and bountiful wildlife. Preservation, Muir suggested, would be for the nation as a whole and in perpetuity, and only the federal government would be able to make this a reality. President Roosevelt was persuaded, and he in turn persuaded Congress to establish what eventually became the National Park Service. The United States provided a model for the rest of the world.

Thanks to John Muir's ardor and President Roosevelt's political persuasion, we now carefully manage our wonderful national parks so that all can enjoy their beauty and splendor.

There is a second great natural resource within our wonderful nation: the *human resource*. Not unlike the despoliation of natural treasures, the human resource was also suffering. Especially in the world of work, management of the human resource was outdated. The government created laws to reduce problems such as child labor, minimum wages, workplace safety, family leave, and more, but government alone cannot change attitudes, traditions, and prejudices.

In the previous chapter, I noted that three significant workplace structures are completely outdated or inadequate: authoritarianism is the predominant model of management; organizations do not have a system for the effective and humane treatment of its employees, even in the twenty-first century; and supervision/management is not viewed as a profession but rather as just a job, no training required.

Core4 addresses these structural inadequacies and proposes alternative paths that can be taken by all organizations.

The first, authoritarianism, which is both outdated and unwanted, should be replaced by a participative management philosophy. Employees at all levels want to participate in the life of their organizations as real people and team members, not just as cogs in a machine. Employees are no longer willing to take orders simply to obey and follow their leaders. They want a real (not artificial) relationship with their managers and other team members. They want honest and trusting relationships that enhance motivation, collaboration, and contribution. Work life can be fun and exciting. Participating openly and honestly in an organization does not merely happen with a new statement of philosophy. Leaders can learn the power of enabling, encouraging, and coaching team members to contribute, which, interestingly, employees want. Change from authoritarian leadership to a participative philosophy is a cultural event for the whole organization. It is more than a quick fix, new technique, or different language.

Participative management, while not authoritarian, is also not democratic. Employees do not decide on the company's hiring policies or business decisions. Management has control and is responsible.

A company with participative management gathers counsel and ideas from its members.

WHY DON'T THEY ASK US?

One day visiting while a steel company, I observed a team meeting. The foreman was explaining to his crew what management wanted them to do about a specific problem.

"What's the issue?" I asked.

"There's a problem with a particular fabrication. We know there's a problem. We also know that this solution won't work very well. Why don't they ask us?"

Later, I met with the company president and asked him why management did not ask for worker input on a solution to the fabrication problem. He said he didn't really know why they didn't ask them, but recognizing the value of that idea, management immediately sought suggestions from the shop employees. The employees developed a proposal to solve the problem. Management critiqued and agreed with their recommendation; the problem was resolved, and the employees eagerly implemented the new plan.

Participative management improves the organization's policies, practices, and results; creates improvement in employee morale and enthusiasm; and promotes a sense of ownership among all team members.

Second, Core4 provides a system for people management. Core4 creates a system of practices that humanize, simplify, and strengthen organizational management beyond the current practice of "Do what is right in your own eyes." Core4 creates an internal coaching plan for the training of all managers/supervisors.

While Core4 was being developed, I observed little in the professional literature regarding a system for people management. Core4's use of a system implies that everyone in the organization is included. Every employee, from new hires to administrative personnel, receives the same consistent, predictable, recordable, and humane management/

supervision. Use of the word *system* might be viewed as a controlling style of authoritarianism, but the Core4 system assures that leader/team member interactions be monitored, supervised, and especially, coached so that strong positive relationships are actually developed, not just hoped for.

The following story demonstrates the case of a well-educated person leading his organization with an inadequate system in place for communication and review and with false assumptions as to the goals and methods employed by key individuals in the conduct of their activities.

WHY HAVE YOU LOST TWO VPs?

A president of a large United Way agency that had departments for health, welfare, and social services of various kinds was well recognized and appreciated. The newspaper reported that one of his vice presidents had left the organization, and then, several days later, it was reported that another vice president was fired.

The president had previously shared his management philosophy with me: "You hire good people, tell them what to do, and turn them loose." With this background, it was with some interest that I asked, "What's this about two vice presidents leaving?"

"The one VP did anything he wanted to do without talking to me about it. He started all kinds of stuff, things that were new, and he did not talk to me about anything."

"But isn't that what you like?"

"Yes, but he went too far."

"What about the second VP?"

"He asked me about everything. He couldn't do anything without asking me. He was in my office every day."

"How does all of this relate to your management philosophy?"

"I'm thinking about it."

The president was trying to avoid authoritarian management which was commendable, but he neglected to recognize the needs of his two vice presidents. These vice presidents differed in personality, style, and expression, but both needed regular one-on-one sessions with their president in order to achieve the best results for the organization and accommodate the personal needs of the individuals.

Both the previous example and the following one illustrate the absence of a clear and consistent system for employee management.

WE HATE ONE ANOTHER

I observed a management team meeting at a manufacturing company with seven people on the team. The agenda was poorly prepared, and the team members minimally participated in a variety of unhelpful ways. At the end of the meeting, I asked one team member, "What's going on in this group?"

"We hate one another!"

"What do you mean?"

"Well, they're trying to do me in, and I don't like them. It's more like warfare than it is anything else."

"How long has this been going on?"

"Ever since I came here two years ago. It's even gotten worse."

"Does your leader know this?"

"Yes."

"What does he do about it?"

"On the one hand, he likes it because he thinks it makes us compete harder, and on the other hand, he doesn't know what to do about it."

What a terrible place to work! Without a humane system for relating to and reconciling conflict, the organization's productivity suffers, as does each team member. It becomes a "disorganization."

We all want to feel important or at least needed. The following plaintive cry for inclusion was an illustration of the lack of a humane system for dealing with employees.

WAITING IN LINE IN A COMPANY DINING ROOM

"I never know what's going on." This employee knew I was a consultant and described how she felt completely out of the loop in the company.

"What would you like?"

She was emphatic. "I see things happening that I know will affect me, and I don't know what's behind the events. It makes me uneasy and uncertain as to my place in the organization. I know I'm not important, but I am a part. It's frustrating to work in a place where I feel like I don't even belong."

Humans have a need to belong to a community. We want to know what is happening in our work community. The better we understand what's going on, the better we can cope with change and the more we will want to contribute.

The humane treatment of employees can sometimes be made more difficult by geography.

THE FARTHER AWAY...

A chief executive officer told me, "My team is scattered from New York to Arizona. They work at home and can care for their children, their spouses, and their personal lives. We can't meet for monthly one-on-one sessions and team meetings." (*When the manager or supervisor meets with a team member individually, it is referred to as a one-on-one.*)

"Having our people scattered across the country gives us a presence in these diverse geographic areas, which is important to our business."

"Do your people ever indicate they miss being together occasionally?"

"Yes, but we can't do that with our current budget."

"I understand that might be true if costs are your only criterion. But do you and your people ever get together from year to year?"

"Oh, yes. We have two sales and one management meeting each year."

"Well, on those three occasions, could you plan one-on-one sessions with each member and a team meeting for all of your members? I would guess you could do this but, of course, motivation is the key."

Core4 sees people as a top value that produces better results, saves time, and increases morale. I have found that these one-on-one sessions (at least twelve per year) can be arranged when value is understood. Some administrators are blind to anything but a focus on the bottom line. They see costs associated with travel but have little or no appreciation for the potential improvement in employee productivity as a result of closer interaction with supervisors and other team members. Team meetings can also be arranged when several are together and others are attending via audio or Skype. The farther individuals are separated geographically, the more they need personal time with their managers/supervisors.

Core4 Practices

The Core4 system has four basic practices for effective people management, which came about as a result of observations such as those reported in the first chapter.

Plan agreement. Each employee (from the chief executive officer to the most recent hire) will have a performance plan, often based on a twelve-month time frame with interim targets. Core4 emphasizes that the agreement between supervisor and employee must be honest, clear, and fairly developed as a cooperative plan for success that both support.

One-on-one trusting relationships. Core4 builds relationships between the manager and his or her team members through trusting, open collaboration, and mutual support, with regularly scheduled one-on-one monitoring and coaching sessions.

Teamwork. Every employee is part of a team, where they feel accepted and supported and contribute to the team's success. Core4 builds cooperation and collaborative team relationships for every employee. Managers and supervisors, of course, are on two teams, one as a leader and one as a team member. The team relationships are based on common goals for the team. Trust grows through well-planned and managed team meetings.

Decision process. The decision-making process is a learning, collaborative proposal process open to all employees and provides an opportunity for learning, critiquing, and coaching.

The Core4 system will be effective when every manager/supervisor, owner, or president employs these four practices designed for collaborative, mutually supportive relationships within the organization.

Management as a Profession

The manager/supervisor role is vital to the organization's success. Employees are often moved into a supervisory role for which they have no training or aptitude. Core4 trains managers/supervisors to behave more professionally, rather than viewing supervision as just a job with more status and a higher salary.

As I watched the Tour de France in July 2009, I observed the roads on which the 180 bikers traveled more than one hundred miles a day at an average speed of twenty-five miles per hour. I bike many of the roads in southeastern Pennsylvania, always needing to watch carefully for cracks, holes, and irregularities in the pavement.

But the roads of France appeared to be smooth, regular, and predictable, making feasible the speeds of those cyclists riding fast and closely packed. I wondered why their roads were so good and our roads had so many imperfections.

Shortly thereafter, I was intrigued to actually find a 1908 article in the Pennsylvania *Harleysville News* that described the highways in France. The author stated that the company that builds a highway in France maintains that roadway for one hundred years as part of the contract. The article continued,

> France does not have the best roads because it has special skill in making them. Nor is it because it has especially large or unusually excellent supplies and materials. The same materials can be found all over the US. French roads are perfect because the road business is a profession, and not a job.

Organizations need well-trained managers/supervisors who are responsible for the best results for the team they lead. The Core4 system provides for every team leader, manager, or supervisor to receive this in-house, hands-on clinical training for their people management. The training includes standards, guidelines, and monitoring to assure consistent treatment of all employees. Training sometimes is taught by a consultant to the organization and sometimes led by a human resources staff member. This process is a quantum leap from the idea that "Everyone does what's right in their own eyes."

A key part of the clinical training process is for managers to observe team members as they lead their own team meetings and as they conduct one-on-one sessions with their individual team members. Supportive observations and coaching are invaluable. Such leadership assures high-quality relationships with improved results and individual satisfaction for both the team member and the supervisor/manager.

In summary, Core4 was developed from a recognition of the need to move beyond the historically entrenched philosophy and methods of authoritarianism. Core4 develops a participative philosophy that more fully meets the human need for inclusion and personal recognition. The four practices of the Core4 system are detailed in the following chapters. It is hoped that you will come to understand the principle detailed in the following story.

CORE4 HAS SOUL

Following one of the Core4 training sessions at an actuarial company, one of the managers said to me, "Core4 has soul."

"What does that mean?"

"This management method allows us, as human beings, to be recognized as individuals. It knows we are important and that what we have to say is of value. It wants us all to be heard."

Soul *is another way of saying "personhood." Honoring one's soul means a lot to all of us.*

Authors don't often suggest to their readers they might enjoy writing in the book they're reading. We've all made marginal comments as we read books of interest. (Hopefully, those jottings were done in books within our personal libraries.) In this book, however, space is provided for you to reflect on what you've just read. Three major observations have been discussed in Chapters 1 and 2. (1) Organizations have been observed as continuing to operate with an authoritarian philosophy and methods. (2) There is no real system for consistent people-management in most organizations. (3) There is little recognition that individuals who are in leadership positions have training in order to succeed in their management/supervisory task.

From the point of view of your employment situation and your knowledge of your own organization, reflect on these major observations as presented in Chapters 1 and 2. Respond to the observations using a two column approach as a way of organizing your thoughts. What are your LIKES and CONCERNS?

A participative philosophy and method replacing authoritarianism.

| LIKES | CONCERNS |

A people-management system replaces no consistent system

<u>LIKES</u>   <u>CONCERNS</u>

In-house training for supervision replacing no training

<u>LIKES</u>   <u>CONCERNS</u>

CHAPTER 3

PRACTICE ONE: PERFORMANCE PLAN
AGREEMENT AND ACCOUNTABILITY

Performance Plan Agreement

E very employee has a task (tasks) to perform in order for the organization to achieve good results. Good management is at the heart of achieving good results. Good management requires a clearly understood agreement and a commitment to the job of each team member, recognizing the high value for both the leader and the team member in the formulation of a plan that is mutually understood and agreed upon (not just assigned). Core4 suggests that worker tasks can be summarized into two to six key performance measures (KPMs). KPMs have a high value for employees in assessing their job performance. For any single KPM, there will be many activities required for those results to be achieved. In order to understand how KPMs are developed for an individual employee, it may be helpful to examine a fictitious work situation with which a specific employee may be faced.

The organization is a clothing manufacturer with divisions for golf, tennis, and fitness. The employee is a salesperson dedicated to golf apparel. The territory in which this individual works is eastern Pennsylvania and New Jersey, excluding the metropolitan area outside New York City. The company had identified, and the sales representative had called on, more than five hundred public and private green-grass facilities, retail golf outlets, and practice facilities (mostly driving ranges). Big-box chain stores are not included in this salesperson's responsibilities. In the preceding year, about half of the private clubs and public facilities had purchased from the company. More than half of the retail outlets were customers, but only a fraction of the practice facilities purchased golf apparel. Total sales for the previous year were $1.2 million.

As the new year approached, Tom, the sales representative, met with his supervisor, Phil, the vice president for marketing (eastern region). The meeting's purpose was to establish the goals (KPMs) for Tom's work in the coming year. They both knew that the total sales for the previous year had been $1.2 million, and so the first part of their discussion was to come to an agreement as to the sales goal for the coming year. After considerable discussion, they came to a mutually agreed-upon decision that the goal for the coming year should be $1.36 million. The most important factor in this decision was that it was a mutually agreed-upon goal.

Having come to that mutual agreement, the first KPM for Tom's year was total volume of sales. The number of sales calls that Tom will make for this year is not a KPM but represents a necessary activity to achieve the agreed-upon KPM.

Tom and Phil then created three additional KPMs. Tom suggested that he wanted to achieve a greater percentage of sales within three of the four types of facilities he serves. He suggested that, for green-grass operations, he would propose a 4 percent increase in sales to private clubs, a 5 percent increase to public facilities, and a 3 percent increase to retail outlets. Those three areas of increased sales represent three additional KPMs. It was Tom's idea that an increase in sales at practice facilities was likely not possible. Phil agreed with Tom's proposed increases.

At the conclusion of this one-on-one meeting, Tom and Phil had agreed on four KPMs for Tom's work in the coming year. Because they had developed these goals in a mutually agreed-upon way, a level of trust and cooperation was realized. Tom was now in a position to establish monthly targets that would lead to year-end results as described in the KPMs.

Phil had similar one-on-one meetings with the five other sales representatives in the eastern region. At the conclusion of those six one-on-one sessions, Phil called a team meeting of the sales reps. Each representative reported his or her sales goals for the coming year to the group. Phil reported on how those sales projections, if achieved, fit into the company's overall plan for the year. Phil also provided the group a schedule of monthly team meetings for the year. He had previously scheduled monthly one-on-one sessions with each of the sales representatives at their first meetings of the year.

The next stop for Phil was a team meeting where he was a member rather than the leader. It was a meeting of all regional vice presidents for marketing (golf). The meeting's purpose was to combine the seven regional sales teams' projections for the coming year. The team meeting results were then forwarded to upper management, where the company's targets for the coming year were finalized. Upper management's decision could require an adjustment to each of the regional team's efforts.

If an organization—any organization—is going to accomplish its mission, then measures that indicate it is achieving its goals (KPMs) must be in place and regularly monitored. If you do not measure results, then chances are good that you will not get them.

YOU GET WHAT YOU MEASURE

"How are things going?"

"Good."

"How do you know?"

"It's a feeling I have, but I think I made my number. My boss knows better than I do."

"Why is that?"

"He sees the real numbers, and I don't."

"What numbers?"

"The ones he is interested in."

"Are you interested in them too?"

"Yes, of course; the ones pertaining to my job."

"Why don't you know?"

"He likes to be one up."

Many team members do not receive accurate, timely feedback on how they are progressing toward their plan day by day or month by month. In Tom's story, he may not be aware of certain events that affect his progress toward achieving positive KPM results. For example, he might not receive notification of a cancelled sale or a sale that is not approved because of the purchaser's negative credit history. This sometimes unconscious, negative, and controlling behavior by a boss reveals a lack of cooperation and results in anxiety for the team member about fulfilling the mutually agreed-upon goals. I learned that when a target is mutually established and the team member is supported in his or her efforts, then that target is usually achieved.

Some nonprofit organizations resist the idea of measuring their work or having targets aimed at achieving goals. Their position is that their work is personal or spiritual or inspirational and hence not measurable. The Core4 response is that these organizations and individuals would realize fulfillment and success with careful development of KPMs and targets with support and regular coaching.

THERE'S ONE THING THAT'S MISSING—LOVE

We were concluding a management training program at a social service facility for the mentally handicapped when one staff member said, "There's one thing missing, and that's love.

"What do you mean by that?"

"We see new staff people hired, and they don't know these clients, and they're actually afraid of them in many cases. Eventually—hopefully—they come to care for them. We don't have any measurement that looks at the care, concern, and love for these clients."

"How important is that?"

"It's actually the most important thing."

"In that case, it's vital that we find a way to include a measure that reflects the care and concern of the staff toward their clients. This, logically, will be a piece of the training program."

Through careful deliberations with the staff, we developed a five-point continuum ranging from fear to acceptance to love into which each staff member could self-describe their attitudes toward the clients whom they served. All staff members used this continuum as its value came to be recognized. Staff discovered that this measurement method was also an excellent training tool for new staff members.

Accountability

Accountability is having a responsibility to another person or group. The team member has a responsibility to his or her supervisor and fellow team members. Everyone is also accountable to the organization as a whole. In the Core4 work environment, the team member and the team leader have a mutual responsibility to each other as well as a shared accountability with fellow team members. Core4 promotes accountability as a way of developing stronger employee morale and greater effectiveness. In some organizations, accountability can be totally missing or viewed with fear and anxiety.

TO WHOM ARE YOU ACCOUNTABLE?

Visiting a college one day, I happened upon a friend who said he was on his way to a committee meeting.

"What committee?" I asked.

"It's the curriculum committee."

"What do you do? It sounds like an important committee."

"Nothing."

"How often do you meet?"

"Monthly."

"What you do in those meetings?"

"We talk for a few minutes and then we go our own way. We never get any assignments. We don't know who to report to, and nobody's ever asked us to do anything."

"How many of you are on this committee?"

"There are eight of us."

"You mean there are eight professors who meet every month with no agenda, no assignments, and no reporting? How long has this been going on?"

"I've been on this committee for three years."

No assignments, no supervision, and a total lack of accountability. Even in a place of higher learning there needs to be careful management to reduce wasted time, lowered morale, and a lack of results.

It is possible to get a sense of accountability within an organization by looking at an organizational chart.

THAT'S NOT THE WAY IT WORKS

I was in Richard's office waiting for him to finish his phone call before going to lunch. I noticed an organizational chart lying on his desk. Being a curious type, I asked, "What's this?"

"It's our company's organizational chart."

"Where are you?" (*That should have been easy. He was a key manager.*)

"I'm not sure, but I think this is me."

"So, it looks like you have six people on your team?"

Sounding a little perturbed, he mumbled, "I don't know if they're on my team or not. We never meet."

Looking over the chart, I asked, "Is this your boss?"

"Yes, he's one of my bosses. I have three."

"Really? Three bosses in practice but only one according to the chart. What's the problem?"

"The chart looks nice, but all I know is that's not the way it works."

Sometimes, organizational charts don't mean much. Ideally, they should reveal team and personal relationships, communication, and accountability within the organization. If relationships within the organization change and are not reflected in the organizational chart, then confusion, a lack of accountability, unclear supervision, and increased anxiety persist.

In summary, agreement on the performance plan between the team member and his or her team leader, with commitment to each other to collaborate in achieving that plan, is the first of the Core4 practices. Using KPMs, the team member is able to focus on monthly targets and to make the plan achievable and enjoyable. The team member is accountable to his or her manager, team, and the organization as a whole.

As was done at the end of Chapter 2, space is now being provided for reflections on Chapter 3: Performance Plan Agreement and Accountability. Reflect on the insights you have regarding your organization. What are your:

LIKES   CONCERNS

CHAPTER 4

PRACTICE TWO: ONE-ON-ONE

WHAT'S THERE TO TALK ABOUT?

I asked a company president, "Do you talk with your people?"

"What's there to talk about? I'm not about to discuss their personal troubles."

"Of course not. But what about work issues?"

"What's there to talk about? They know their jobs!"

The surprising thing is that this leader's approach is more the rule than the exception. Sometimes, managers/supervisors do not know how to ask questions about the work process without being critical or demeaning. They are unaware of the power of support, coaching, and caring.

The relationship between the manager/supervisor and the individual team member may be the most important component of a successful work environment. A poor relationship with the boss is a high cause of employee dissatisfaction, weak performance, and even departure. Chapter 3 presented the structures and methods for creating strong, honest, supportive, and genuine relationships.

Once both parties agree on the job, they will then determine how to assure progress toward the completion of that task. Key performance measures (KPMs) are developed and will be reviewed at each one-on-one session.

The real relationship between team leader and team member and the relationship with fellow team members are the essential factors in good people management. The workplace is harmed and diminished by weak, artificial, manipulative, anxious, fearful, and even hostile leadership. Core4 is a system that provides simple structures and methods for creating strong, trusting, honest, supportive, and genuine relationships.

Manager/Member Relationships

The team leader and team member plan to monitor progress on completion of agreed-upon targets with a well-planned schedule, a year in advance, for these one-on-one meetings.

The purposes of the one-on-one meetings are to create genuine, honest, and trusting relationships between the leader and the team member, assuring meaningful results and fulfillment. With a schedule of (typically) at least monthly one-on-one sessions, the leader and team member will avoid the surprise of unexpected problems. One-on-one meetings will provide a continuity of coaching and support, helping the team member grow in his or her ability to complete expected tasks and contribute meaningfully to the team's goals.

Several days prior to a scheduled one-on-one meeting, the leader should confirm the session time and review the agenda, which is primarily to examine the team member's performance plan. The team member may add to the agenda.

- The leader begins the session by asking the team member what has gone well in the previous month and affirms the team member's efforts accordingly.
- Based on the agreed-upon key performance plan, the team member presents his or her past month's activity by way of the

KPM review, with year-to-date progress, cause(s) of variance (if any), and a plan for correction.

- The leader's encouragement, support, coaching, and praise will cause the team member to respond with appreciation, increased motivation, and a desire for fulfillment. The listening/speaking ratio for the session should be approximately 80 percent team member to 20 percent leader.

- Planning ahead for next month's actions will reduce the need for drop-in "Have you got a minute?" sessions. The goal of the monthly one-on-one sessions is problem prevention and plan achievement.

- Review any other agenda items. Both the leader and the team member will keep notes on these meetings regarding the fulfillment of agreed-upon planned efforts.

- Inquire about the team member's relationship with peers, and review the team member's report to the team at the next team meeting.

- If the team member is the leader of a team of his or her own, then the team member will review that team's functioning and report each month on one specific team member and his or her ongoing relationships. Coaching is vital at this point.

- Confirm next month's session, and again praise the team member's efforts.

I FORGOT

I worked in a psychiatric center that had a very competent, successful executive director, Bob, who was my immediate supervisor. My position entailed starting a new department, and I had several ideas that I wanted to implement. I needed Bob's approval and asked to get together.

He welcomed that idea and, at his suggestion, we met in a local bar in midafternoon. I had no problem with that; it would be quiet, away from telephones and other distractions. We had a healthy discussion, and I asked him if we could meet in a couple weeks so that he would have time to think and provide answers to my development questions.

At our next session two weeks later, I asked Bob about my questions. Bob had not taken notes—it was quite dark in the bar—but he had promised to have a response to those specific items for me at this meeting.

Bob was embarrassed. "I'm sorry. I forgot."

"Bob, what am I going to do? You've got to write things down! When will you give me an answer?"

Conversations and meetings between boss and employee are important for achieving agreement and progress, but I frequently find that such meetings are a waste of time. To meet in a bar possibly signaled a poor plan because clear records and notes should be taken and followed up by both the team member and the leader.

I was confused. My "good" boss was poorly organized. I was surprised that I needed to remind him of what seemed a simple management function: keeping notes and fulfilling his promise of a response to questions. Moreover, I saw he had no clear or consistent method for managing me, even when I asked for his help. He "forgot."

The one-on-one sessions between team leader and team member should be comfortable and rewarding as the month's work is reviewed. Criticizing is not useful. Coaching and support are vital. Having the team member focus on his or her KPM targets for each month and preparing the KPM review provides a basis for the team member to clearly understand his or her task and how to keep up the agreed-upon pace in order to meet the year's goals. Sometimes, the team member may need additional coaching as part of the solution, and so it should be arranged.

Core4 suggests a midyear one-on-one session where an additional topic is "Let's talk about us." This can be both a rewarding and a challenging event for the leader. Guidelines for this session have the leader asking the team member questions concerning his or her perception of the leader's effectiveness. If the leader has been given good, constructive supervision during his or her clinical training prior to becoming a supervisor, then he or she will approach this session with eagerness. The leader will have already had this same discussion with the leader of the team on which he or she is a member.

The manager will begin by asking the team member, "What do you appreciate about my management?" Other questions will include "What do you want from me?" "What can I do that will help?" "What do you wish I did differently?" "What do I do that hinders your efforts?" and "What can I do to improve our work together?" The manager and the team member will have achieved a level of trust, and the team member will feel comfortable in answering these questions in an honest, straightforward manner.

The second half of the session focuses on the team member's work. Again, trust is being built as the team member is given time to talk about himself or herself. Questions include "What are two things you feel you are doing well in your job?" "What parts of your job do you dislike or want to improve?" and "Are there barriers that stand in the way of your productivity?" Ideally, this one-on-one session will be a learning experience for both the leader and the team member. The better it is done, the more this session will build trust as the manager exposes himself or herself to a bit of personal risk.

TRY IT. YOU'LL LIKE IT

I conducted a Core4 program with a newspaper in northern Indiana. The newspaper editors and managers were educated and very vocal in expressing their ideas. We had a lot of interactions, and it appeared as though everyone was buying into the practices of Core4 until we got to the "Let's talk about us" section. The copy editor said, "I don't need this with my people. Some of them have worked for me for twenty years, and all of them have been here for at least ten. I know them really well, and some are even social friends. We work very well together."

I stood my ground. "You have come to like the Core4 program, and you trust me, so I urge you to try this; I think you'll like it." I finished that training session hoping, but not knowing, if he would follow through.

At my next session with him alone, he was eager to report on his interviewing. He said, "I was totally surprised. I thought I knew my people, but Jimmy and I met after work for his one-on-one and we talked for four hours. I learned stuff about me and about him and about the newspaper that I never knew! The same thing happened with all of the other interviews: two to four hours each. It was amazing. This interview method is worth the entire cost of the program. We've learned so much, and we're a much better team because of it. Thank you."

I was blown away! Tears and cheering followed his presentation.

In the typical Core4 process, the manager is the driving force behind the initiation and implementation of one-on-one meetings. There can be occasions when roles are reversed, and it is the member who is managing the manager.

MANAGING YOUR BOSS

A fifty-bed hospital was owned and operated by a for-profit corporation that appointed a new president to manage the facility. He had taken over day-to-day management two months earlier.

All department heads dealt directly with the president. Early on, the head of social services, Kris, recognized a problem with Bill's management style. He appeared to be insecure in his role as leader of the institution and gave lots of contradictory orders that created unnecessary work for everyone. Kris, an eight-year hospital employee, sought guidance regarding issues she was experiencing with recently instituted state regulations. Each time she approached Bill, he indicated that he was too busy to deal with her at that time but to "See me later."

Kris was a believer in the Core4 system for the workplace. She had often talked with two other department heads, Phyllis, the director of nursing services, and Dorrie, chief dietitian for the hospital, about their impressions of Bill's management style. Kris proposed an idea of how the three of them might be able to manage their manager.

She asked Bill if she could buy him coffee at Appleby's, located across the street from the hospital, at three the following afternoon. She suggested this off-site location in order to minimize distractions and requested thirty minutes to discuss "our mutual interest in being compliant with the new state regulations."

To her relief, Bill agreed. On their walk to the restaurant, Kris asked the president how he was enjoying his role at the hospital. She also inquired about his feelings toward the community and how his family was settling in. Small talk, yes, but an initial step toward achieving trust and respect.

Coffee was ordered and served. Over the next thirty minutes, Kris asked questions about how they should respond to the state's directives. That half hour was divided into about twenty minutes of Bill's thoughts and ten minutes of Kris asking questions or requesting clarifications of his ideas.

Respecting the agreed-upon thirty-minute schedule, Kris brought the discussion to an end with a sincere thanks to Bill for talking with her. She asked if they might do this again in two weeks, during which time she would reflect on his ideas and come up with some possible solutions for the challenges facing the hospital on the basis of the new state regulations. Bill said he'd be happy to do this again. "I appreciated you asking me to consult with you on those important issues facing your department."

Kris reported to her two fellow department heads her impressions about the meeting with Bill. Two weeks later, they crossed the street to the restaurant and ordered coffee. This time, Kris did more talking and shared with Bill her ideas concerning the revised state regulations. After some give-and-take, they came to a mutual agreement as to how Kris should deal with the situation.

Once again, Bill expressed his appreciation to Kris for working with him in the activities of her department. He indicated that he wished more of the department heads would take the initiative to talk with him about their situations.

Phyllis and Dorrie received Kris's report of her talks with Bill with great interest. They both decided that they would approach Bill individually about meeting him for a short one-on-one session as a way of introducing him to their departments' issues.

Happily, they both were successful in initiating the new president into their needs and concerns during those one-on-one sessions. The entire staff noticed changes in Bill's management style.

While courage is required to bring about change in a supervisor's management style, and although it was not a total solution to his leadership efforts, Kris and the two other department heads were successful in managing their manager in order to improve their results and work life. Kris came by her knowledge of the Core4 system honestly; after all, she's my daughter.

In summary, the one-on-one sessions are scheduled for a whole year in order to avoid communication only when there is a problem. The leader should be generous in his or her praise of the team member's efforts as they jointly work to stay on track toward completion of their agreed-upon goals.

REACHING FOR THE SUN

We had a five-foot wall around the small backyard of our city residence. Looking outside one day, I thought it would be fun to plant tulips that, in the spring, would make that dreary corner beautiful. The tulips did finally blossom, but they lay on the ground growing in an easterly direction.

They were growing toward the sun, which would lighten their corner of the yard for only a few minutes each day. Those tulips did blossom, and they were lovely, but they lay on the ground with their heads raised.

I was reminded that people are like my tulips in at least one way: they will do almost anything for warm words of encouragement and praise, like my tulips seeking the sun.

As you surely know, one-on-one sessions can be rewarding, but also frustrating. Again you are provided space to reflect on the Core4 suggestions as read in this chapter and express your:

LIKES   CONCERNS

CHAPTER 5

Practice Three: The Team and Teamwork

A team is a group of people working together toward the same goal. Membership on a team provides a home base where the employee is accepted, unafraid, and appreciated for the efforts he or she puts forth for the organization. Being a member of such an association is essential to a good work life and can also be lots of fun, but it is difficult to achieve when authoritarian management is directing traffic. Teamwork cannot be assured if leadership is not supporting and coaching the process. As previously indicated, Core4 plans that every employee has membership on a team.

IT'S NOT A TEAM—JUST A BUNCH

A friend was owner and president of a small and rapidly growing furniture company. During the course of a tour, I asked if he worked with a management team.

"Not exactly, but a group of us get together every Monday morning for breakfast. These are the guys who really know what's going on."

"Who's in the group?"

"My brother, who's our company engineer; my cousin, the salesman; the janitor, my dad; and sometimes others drop in if there's something they need our help with."

"What do you do at these meetings?"

He described how they talk over specific problems, look forward to the coming week, and what they might expect. "Mostly, though, it's just a good time around breakfast. It's not a team but rather a bunch of us that get together weekly. We've been doing this a long time, and we enjoy it."

People (workers) want, enjoy, and need teams to collaborate on the work of the organization. Many leaders are unaware of how much they gain by employing the team concept that includes every person in the organization as part of a small team that has a clearly defined function and works together to complete their goals.

WHAT DO YOU MEAN SHE'S NOT ON THE TEAM?

I asked a company president who was on his team. He named four or five vice presidents, but there was no secretary, administrative assistant, or support staff, even though I saw those people in his outer office.

"What about your administrative assistant?"

"No, she's not on the team."

"Why is that?"

"Well, she doesn't really know anything about our product or processes. She just does what we tell her to do."

"Is this true throughout the organization: administrative assistants are not on the management teams?"

"They're never on the team because they aren't really in on what's happening."

I said, "Are you kidding? They likely know more than you do about what's going on in the organization and why things work and don't work."

Composition of the team is often not rational or mindful of what's best for the organization. Even today, after some improvement, many people still do not have a team relationship where their roles and contributions to the organization are recognized.

In the experience of Core4, teams are best if they consist of no more than eight members.

DYING TO TALK

Very few people were willing or interested in talking at a team meeting I observed. After the team leader left, several of us were standing around, and I asked one of them what they thought about the meeting.

"It was just like usual. Not very much happens."

"Why not?"

"We don't know what to say. Many times, the boss gets angry or he says he doesn't want to talk about that now. It's frustrating."

"I'm dying to talk," said another of the participants. "There are all kinds of things I'd like to say, but that meeting's not the place to say it."

"Where is the place to say it?" I asked.

"There's no place. But I've got plenty to talk about, and I think it would be important to the organization. I know it would be important to me, but the boss is not a listener. He doesn't want to hear us."

Most human beings want to talk and tell their stories, share their experiences, and be listened to. There are few good listeners and lots of talkers. Bosses would profit greatly by listening, asking good questions, and hearing what their employees are saying. Some people, however, are fearful of embarrassment or criticism. They will require special help from their team leaders to develop a comfort level with this process.

I DON'T GET TO TALK

I became the fifth member of the executive director's team at the psychiatric center where I worked. Our team of five members, plus the director, expanded during the next two years to include twelve members. I recognized that I didn't talk much in our team meetings. Actually, no one had much time to talk. If everyone took just five minutes, an hour would have passed, and we would not have had time for anything approaching an in-depth discussion of any issue, let alone other agenda items.

Bob, our executive director, was approachable, so I wasn't hesitant to tell him that I didn't like being on the team. Of course he was surprised, as this was the top management group. "What's wrong?" he asked.

"I don't get time to talk. Even you don't talk. I expect you have another, smaller, group where you do talk."

"How do you know that?" he asked.

I admitted that I didn't know but only suspected.

He confirmed the existence of a smaller group. "I found that with the larger group I didn't have an opportunity to present my ideas, nor did the other members have time to share their thoughts. A small group allows flexibility of content and in-depth exploration." He asked me to join that smaller team.

In addition to the need for trust, commitment to one another is a critical dynamic within the team. Each member wants to feel that all team members are fully committed to working toward the team's targets.

Accountability is the measure of the team's effectiveness. If one team member is having trouble, then it is important that he or she asks for help from the other team members, as well as the leader, in order for his or her individual goals to be achieved. To call for help is better than being defensive and hoping that his or her difficulties are not exposed. When team members support one another, positive results are more likely to occur.

In his book *The Five Dysfunctions of a Team*, Patrick Lencioni describes dysfunction within a team and suggests that the most important shortcoming is lack of trust. Trust is critical to teamwork and is one of the leader's key tasks. The leader's job is to build trust with each team member as well as among the team members themselves. Core4 says it this way: "Trust cannot be demanded or expected; it is earned. The leader needs to prove trustworthy by never betraying, criticizing, or demeaning anyone behind their backs, in a public forum, or even in private. Such high standards for organizational leadership build trust and teamwork."

Lencioni speaks to conflict in the life of any team. Many fear conflict because they do not know how to cope with emotions and challenges. Core4 recognizes two sources of conflict. One has to do with personality and ego struggles within a competitive environment. Fears over a team member's status and recognition can prevail. Ego and status conflicts are best resolved in 1 + 1 sessions with the leader offering praise and recognition and disallowing those conflicts to interfere with team achievement.

The second source involves strategic conflicts where the focus is on what is best for the team. Conflicts are best dealt with through leader confidence and without prejudice, reinforcing collaboration and enhancing team spirit.

There are five possible approaches to solving conflict within a team:

- The competing or authoritarian resolution: I win, you lose.
- The avoiding resolution: I lose, you lose.
- The accommodating resolution: I lose, you win.
- The compromising solution: a small win for you, and a small win for me.
- The collaborative resolution: it works for both of us; it's a win-win.

Obviously, the collaborative resolution is best but may take longer to achieve. Short-term solutions can be gained with an authoritarian directive, but typically, this type of resolution is viable for a limited time only.

Team Meetings

The quality of leadership may be most clearly revealed in team meetings. Core4 finds that team meetings that have a clear, agreed-upon agenda do better than those without an agenda.

WHATCHA GOT?

I frequently asked if I could sit in on a company's team meeting. In one such meeting, the leader's initial words were: "Whatcha got?"

A couple people reported about a situation with which they were dealing. The meeting was slow. It ended thirty minutes later.

"What was the purpose of that meeting?" I asked the leader.

"Well, I want them to feel that they can ask any questions and that they can discuss things, and it's just good to get them all together."

The team members said that the meetings did not offer much value. They liked getting together because they frequently had not seen other team members since the previous meeting, and they enjoyed that social aspect. But except in situations where big company changes were announced, the meetings themselves were useless. Having the team leader ask "Whatcha got?" is an insulting effort at trying to build teamwork. These employees need to hear from one another and from their leader about progress on plans. That did not happen. The important process of assuring one another that year-to-date targets were being reached and supporting and encouraging one another did not happen. Individual accountability was not clear, and for many, there was little focus on the goals for achievement. Monitoring the progress toward meeting goals was almost impossible.

Without an agenda, the team recognizes that the team leader has little use for the meeting and also the team. Core4 uses the team meeting as a key to success and joy.

WHAT HAPPENS IN THE HUDDLE?

I enjoy weekend afternoon football games, and at halftime of one particular game, I got to thinking about teams and teamwork.

I observed the team come to a huddle before each play and focused on what was happening in the huddle. It was indeed a team meeting and had the same basic agenda every time. I summarized the agenda as past, present, and future.

The quarterback (team leader) might yell at the tight end, "Didn't you realize you were the hot receiver?" (*A piece of the past.*)

"Now it's third down and four, and they're rushing me like crazy." (*This is the present.*)

"Our next play is Alabama left, thirty-four, on two." (*All right, team. This is our future course of action.*)

The huddle is a visible, simple illustration of the need for a team to report on both past successes and failures, assess the status of the conditions as they are at the present, and plan for the next steps—the future.

Without training in the conduct of team meetings, leaders are often unaware of the value that can be gained in these sessions. Some leaders view these meetings as an obligation which they dislike and avoid because they do not know what to do. Leaders must be taught to conduct team meetings employing the dynamic three agenda topics: reviewing the past and the associated successes and failures, considering the present status of the team's goals, and looking to the future with specific strategies for change if they are needed. Members should also be given an opportunity to report on their own progress.

Team meetings work best if scheduled (typically) monthly and in advance for the entire year. Prior to the scheduled event, the leader should distribute an agenda and indicate how long the meeting will last. Usually two hours is a maximum for success. Meetings should rarely be canceled. Attendance is expected for every member at every meeting, but if a team member is unable to attend, then he or she should send a substitute to take his or her place. The team member or leader who is going to be absent should prepare his or her stand-in on what to expect and provide an overview of the agenda. This becomes a great learning experience for the stand-in and gives the team and the absent team member another opportunity to mentor.

Dynamic three agenda: the basic structure for the agenda of every team meeting is the dynamic three: past, present, and future. While not a fixed ratio, the best distribution of time allotted to the three is 20 percent, 20 percent, and 60 percent.

The location for team meetings should be a pleasant place without interruptions.

IS THIS WHERE YOU HAVE YOUR TEAM MEETINGS?

In becoming acquainted with a large steel company, I asked if I could visit a team meeting. I was referred to a welding team.

"We don't really have team meetings. We get together on an as-needed basis."

I met with them at the agreed-upon place with overhead equipment moving in several directions. It was noisy and dirty, and we were standing where equipment and people were coming and going. Finally, the leader called for attention.

"Now settle down and hear this." He read a memorandum from the "big bosses."

Later, I asked why we were meeting in the middle of all this manufacturing.

"We don't have any place else to hold a meeting."

"Couldn't you find an office?"

"There aren't any offices in this building."

Space for getting together is necessary for team meetings to be successful. Later, this company became a client, and the lack of adequate space for supervision and team meetings resulted in the erection of a large addition to the plant, with offices for managers and team meetings.

The team leader will request contributions for the upcoming agenda. Suggestions from the team can advance the group's spirit by recommending agenda inclusions that may not have occurred to the leader. The agenda and proposals are circulated in advance of the meeting for good preparation. Team members review proposals and identify their likes and concerns prior to the meeting. Such preparation assures that the meeting will be productive and that each team member will participate in the meeting, realizing it was successful and they were rewarded for having been there.

The team leader directs the meeting, assuring that each agenda item is completed and that each team member speaks and participates in the discussions. Leadership means securing participation and collaboration. Frequently, follow-up on an agenda item is needed, and the leader will be clear as to who will follow up and when. Team leaders engage participation but do not dominate group meetings.

Notes (minutes) are taken for each team meeting, indicating how all agenda items were addressed. The notes, which are compiled by a team member (in collaboration with the leader), are distributed to every team member two or three days following the meeting. Minutes should be short, usually no more than one page. Additional pages may be needed for exhibits and/or proposals.

The Boys in the Boat (2013) is a best-selling nonfiction book describing the 1936 Olympics and the rowing competition by the team from Washington State University. The teamwork of these eight oarsmen and the coxswain was so well developed that all members were fully and wholeheartedly giving their all to stay in an exact rhythm with one another, providing the most efficient passage of the scull through sometimes choppy water. It is a well-written story of ultimate teamwork.

The team and teamwork are essential to the Core4 management system. How does your organization deal with this vital component to its success? What are your:

LIKES   CONCERNS

CHAPTER 6

PRACTICE FOUR: DECISION MAKING

O ne question I asked regularly when interviewing an organiza-tion is: "How do you make decisions here?" Often, with rolled eyes, employees will point up and say decisions come from top management. Sometimes, they say they really don't know how deci-sions are made.

Organization leaders and managers themselves often said they could not really describe how decisions were made. When people have little or no involvement in the decision-making process, they will be slow and ineffective in the implementation of those decisions.

Books have been written about the decision-making process. This chapter, and Core4's approach to decision making, is not meant to be a definitive statement on the importance of this aspect of the organi-zation's function. Core4's emphasis looks at how employees can be involved in this management prerogative.

Core4's participative management gathers contributions from all team members for the good of the organization and its people. The sug-gestion box, also known as the bitch box, is not effective for change or decision making and greatly demeans the concept of real human beings collaborating to make decisions that are good for all.

Another weak effort to improve an organization's function takes the form of "Let me throw this idea on the table." It is admitting not much thought has been given to the idea, but maybe someone else can pick it up and make it work.

Sometimes, leaders squelch ideas by immediately questioning the team member's suggestion.

THAT'S A GREAT IDEA, BUT...

"Joe, I've got a great idea!"

"Great! Let's hear it, Mike."

The team member, Mike, describes his idea.

"That's interesting, but have you thought about...?"

The boss's comments reflect skepticism of the employee's "great idea" and squelch further discussion. Team members learn not to offer ideas because of the resistance received in prior efforts. Frequently, the ideas were not well thought out, but the leader's reaction discouraged them. It would be much better to coach the team member in order to improve these efforts and contributions. This may sound counterintuitive because you would think leaders would want to explore new options. Unfortunately, the status quo is a primary motivator in most organizations.

The Decision Process

Brainstorming often is useful in presenting an idea to the team. The team member can request a few minutes for brainstorming to give a quick view to the team prior to development of a formal proposal. The presenter asks what aspects of the presenter's ideas the team likes or has concerns about. The supervisor and each team member respond with both likes and concerns. This process will provide a good sense of support, within the team, for the presenter's idea. This process contributes additional ideas from a different perspective. The team member and team leader will be better prepared to develop a proposal based on this preliminary participation.

Core4 provides a proposal format to guide the team member and leader in developing the idea's concept, plan, options, and accountability. Developing an idea into a proposal requires some thought and research but really is not difficult. Assisting a team member in developing a proposal gives the team leader a valuable opportunity to coach and support. Developing a proposal allows the team member to gain a broader knowledge of the organization's purposes and methods. Developing and presenting a proposal for critique by a manager or leader provides excellent feedback on and understanding of how implementation may be achieved within the organization.

Critique

Once a proposal is prepared, with supporting documents as needed, it will be presented to the team in detail. Team members should receive the proposal several days ahead of the meeting in order to study it carefully before the critiquing process. Each team member will again state his or her likes and concerns about the proposal. A record of each of the likes and concerns should be maintained in such a way that all members can visually see all comments as they are made. A white board is useful for this purpose. As they review the likes and concerns, the team discussion typically reveals whether the proposal seems fully acceptable, needs revision, or is not acceptable. Management still has the final decision, of course, but they know how the team feels about the proposal, and they recognize the level of the team's commitment to it.

TWO ARE BETTER THAN ONE

One day, early in my career, I had a good idea about development in my department and spoke to my manager. He heard me out and had several excellent ideas that I hadn't considered. I reflected on his ideas and recognized that they were good and added to my thinking. I was confident I knew that what I was suggesting was good, but he had a different perspective.

The value of the external perspective is obvious. An individual cannot have both an internal and an external perspective. Having both is better than having only one.

73

Authoritarianism is the most significant deterrent to effective decision making in an organization, and it is seen everywhere. Occasionally, however, a glimmer of participative common sense shines through.

NO RAISES THIS YEAR

That was the announcement made at the psychiatric center shortly after I was hired. I wasn't expecting a raise, but that statement surely started talk among the staff. A group of staff members asked administration why. Administration cited problems, but the most important was that not all staff members were meeting their billing quotas each week.

The staff had no clearly understood standard for billable hours each week. We knew our own production, in general, but there had been little communication about the relationship between client billings and the budget.

Drilling down a little deeper revealed that two key department heads were not meeting their quotas. Administration's position was that staff members should have twenty-four billable hours each week to make our budget. The two department heads were producing sixteen.

Defending their positions, the two department heads suggested they were doing high-quality counseling, which required more preparation and review, and they could not meet the twenty-four-hour target.

Working together, staff and administration developed a solution. The consensus was that the department heads had some administrative responsibilities as legitimate replacement for billable hours, but there was little sympathy for the idea that the quality of counseling done by these two individuals was higher than that done by other staff members.

Failure to communicate is a common authoritarian mistake. In this story, employees inserted themselves into the decision-making process by asking for more information. Management listened to the employee concerns and an accommodation was reached. Too often in the strict authoritarian mode, management does not take the time to listen to employee concerns. In this case, the two department heads refused to meet the standards and were terminated.

Employees can participate in decisions affecting the organization either by critiquing others' proposals or by writing proposals that the employee develops and presents to management. In either case, that participation gives the employee ownership in the organization. The key factor is that the employee was involved in the process. Regardless of whether the organization accepts the team member's proposal, the employee recognizes that his or her proposal received a fair hearing.

In Chapter 6 the Core4 vision contends the organization, be it profit making or not-for-profit, can make the decision making process a participatory experience with all employees involved. Is your organization working that way? How do you view this model and what are your:

LIKES   CONCERNS

CHAPTER 7

SUMMARY

T he development of Core4 (previously called the Greenfield Management System) grew out of my awareness of how management of an organization's employees can be made better. The system is logical, relatively easy to implement, and promotes a work environment that appreciates its workers as worthwhile human beings as well as contributors to the good results of the organization.

Core4 was developed as a correction of three structural shortcomings seen in every organization I observed:

1. authoritarian leadership, long outdated and unwanted
2. inconsistent and inadequate management of employees
3. management/supervision of people that was unprofessional in its practice, with no replicable standards or clinical training

Core4 replaces these structural shortcomings by creating:

1. a participative philosophy of management that replaces ineffective authoritarianism
2. a people-management system that engages every employee from the president to the newly hired

3. a set of practices that eliminates the default position of allowing all managers/supervisors to do whatever feels right and replaces it with professional-style clinical training and standards

The four practices of the Core4 management system are:

1. an agreed-upon performance plan for the work of every employee in the organization, developed collaboratively with each manager and each team member
2. individual, regular interaction with the manager/supervisor called one-on-one
3. belonging to and working with a team for mutual support, encouragement, and satisfaction with higher results
4. participating in the organization's proposal-led decision-making processes

You may recall the story in chapter 1 where the business owner stated, "Who am I to tell them how to manage their people?" That owner was typical of most organization leaders I observed. Without a humane people management system, workers will recognize that their bosses undervalue them. Core4 does not allow managers/supervisors to "Do what is right in their own eyes." Becoming a manager or supervisor requires more. Supervisors/managers need clinical training that is specific to dealing with people.

Although the training of a surgeon is not fully analogous to that of a supervisor or manager, certainly a clinical training requirement seems obvious.

HOW DOES A SURGEON LEARN SURGERY?

A surgeon's training begins with academic study: biology, chemistry, anatomy, and various other disciplines. Next there is the hands-on work with a cadaver where the book-learned anatomy becomes a reality. Then the student spends hours of observation

watching a skilled surgeon performing a host of surgical procedures. Finally, the student starts his or her career in the surgical theater, under the watchful eye of a mentor. Only after the
teacher is satisfied with the student's performance is he or she
prepared to become a practitioner of the craft.

*In interviews with department heads and managers, I always ask
about the effectiveness of that individual's academic training in the
management of people. That question, however phrased, almost always
meets with a vacant stare. "My MBA taught me to analyze financial reports, predict trends in the business cycle, develop strategies for
growth, and even understand human resource's role and responsibilities.
Learning about the specific management of individuals on a one-on-
one basis and in a group setting—not so much."*

There you have it.

Hopefully, as you followed my journey and the accompanying stories, you too have come to see how inadequate and outdated management continues to be. The three structural shortcomings are the tallest
of the hurdles standing in the way of a workplace that seeks to achieve
fulfillment and joy for its employees. I hope that you have recognized—
as did I—that the individuals doing the management were not bad people; as a group, they were usually good, hardworking, honest individuals
unable to move to a different way of doing things.

You have reviewed my assessment of people management in organizations today as I proposed the four practices of Core4 to excite,
improve, and create a great organization. Some leaders may want to
experiment and incorporate only one of the practices initially. That
likely will be valuable, but the four together support one another and
magnify the effects.

Earlier, there was a discussion of human resources in the organization. The value of human resources in dealing with matters of
payroll, leave time, insurance, and benefits is vital. For larger organizations, much of these routine activities may be outsourced, and human

resources specialists are given more responsibility in the care of the organization's people. Installation of the Core4 system, however, will not be initiated through the efforts of human resources. Core4 must be implemented from the top. The owner (chief executive officer) must recognize the program's value as it relates to his or her organization and must bring Core4 into every relationship of the operation. The owner must have a strong personal self-awareness that recognizes his or her own needs as a manager of employees.

Core4 requires discipline. I have encountered criticism from managers/supervisors that it is a time-consuming system. I recognize that perception but suggest that, as the organization moves from problem solving to problem prevention, managers/supervisors will discover that they are freed up from the constant need to put out brush fires. When fully implemented, the manager will be responsible for one team meeting in which he or she is the leader, one team meeting in which he or she is a member, and one one-on-one appointment for each team member, approximately monthly. Granted, this is likely a minimum, but it is a baseline and can be an efficient way to achieve good results.

WHAT DO I DO WITH MY TIME NOW?

A hospital administrator told me he had an open-door policy and was bemoaning the demands that were put on his time. Following the implementation of Core4, as well as a series of training sessions, he established regular, monthly, one-on-one meetings with each team member. The team itself met on a monthly basis. Part of that team effort was to encourage members to help one another through informal interactions.

The manager asked me some months later what he should do with all his extra time. He was both organized and disciplined. The hospital was running more smoothly, as employees learned that they could solve some of their own problems without constantly running to him for help.

During the transition from problem solving to problem prevention,
the administrator was deeply engaged. The end result, however, justified
the short-term discomfort, as he so aptly testified.

In this short book I have suggested that people management has not kept pace with technologic advancements. Management/supervision is not significantly different today than it was in 1950. Core4, I suggest, can ameliorate much of the drudgery that is so often associated with the work environment. Achieving worker satisfaction in the workplace will accomplish two things simultaneously: employees will have a feeling of inclusion and fulfillment, and the organization will achieve improved results.

In the long flow of history, many developments have occurred for the improvement of human life. We have abolished slavery, improved the role and responsibilities of women, and made great advances in medical understanding and treatment. Our daily lives have been enriched with better housing, food, and transportation. Many improvements have occurred in the workplace with mechanization, safety, and computerization, but the management of people has not been improving alongside these advances. It is high time that changes for the betterment of human beings occur. Core4 can help show the way.

Consider now the totality of what you have read. Would the Core4 management system, or some portions of it, work for your organization? Take time to reflect, and if you are interested in sharing your thoughts with the author, please do so. Evaluating the Core4 management system as a whole, what are your:

LIKES   CONCERNS

POSTSCRIPT

This book is the story of how Core4 came about. It is not intended to be a how-to guide. Implementing Core4's practices, cultures, and systems is best done with the assistance of a certified Core4 adviser. Typically, I helped organizations install the Core4 management system by eight-to-ten, monthly, two-day training sessions. The reason for the extensive time and attention given to the installation process was that the participative management philosophy and methods are usually a cultural change from the authoritarian (or authoritarian denial) status of the organization. Turning your organization into a disciplined, happier environment with participation at all levels requires change of management practices, careful review, and reinforcement over time. You can begin these for practices yourself and much can be accomplished with a dedicated, persistent following of the methods. Seeking a consultant to assist with implementation is recommended.

For information on how to engage a Core4 adviser, please see https://Core4.com, and contact James Landis, president of Core4, to discuss your particular situation. He can be reached via email at James@Core4.com or 717 413-7799.

The author and Dr. Fricke can be reached by email at the below addresses.

Chester A. Raber, PhD   craber51@gmail.com
James E. Fricke, PhD   JFricke@ptd.net

ACKNOWLEDGMENTS

I have been blessed with family and friends who have been especially supportive of this project and who have read this manuscript and given excellent counsel: Ed Brubaker, Alan Giagnocavo, Melvin Goering, Gerry Gorelick, Dale High, Steve High, Norm Kauffmann, Jean Kilheffer-Hess, Ed Nangle, Christine Traini, and Bob Wyble. Encouragement and advice also came from my son-in-law, Kevin Holsapple; my daughter, Kris Raber; my brother, Merrill Raber; and my wife and best friend, Gerry Raber.

James Landis, president of Core4, Inc., has made many contributions to this effort and is a strong proponent of this book, as it will contribute to the marketing of Core4 to receptive organizations.

Jim Fricke began his contributions first as a technical support adviser, but with his background in education, he became Special Assistant, which included editing and managing the manuscript development. Without him, this book would not have happened.

Finally, I acknowledge my deepest appreciation for Gerry's support and critical suggestions at key times. Her patience and love are boundless.

REFERENCES

Brown, Daniel James. 2013. *The Boys in the Boat: Nine Americans and Their Epic Quest for Gold at the 1936 Berlin Olympics*. New York: Penguin Group.

Friedman, Ron. 2014. *The Best Place to Work: The Art and Science of Creating an Extraordinary Workplace*. New York: Penguin Group.

Green, Stephen. 2010. *Good Value: Reflections on Money, Morality, and an Uncertain World*. New York: Atlantic Monthly Press.

1908. *Harleysville News*. Unfortunately, this article has been misplaced.

Lencioni, Patrick. 2002. *The Five Dysfunctions of a Team: A Leadership Fable*. San Francisco: Jossey-Bass.

Oxford Dictionary of English. 3rd ed. 2010. Oxford: Oxford University Press.

Suttie, Jill. 2015. "What Makes a Great Workplace?" *Greater Good*, February 25. Accessed August 18, 2016. http://greatergood. berkeley.edu/article/item/what_makes_a_great_workplace.

Zimbardo, Philip. 2007. *The Lucifer Effect: Understanding How Good People Turn Evil*. New York: Random House.